A DARK AND SPLENDID MASS

WORKS BY MARI EVANS

POETRY

Where Is All the Music (Heritage)
I Am a Black Woman (Morrow)

JUVENILES

I Look at Me (Third World)
J.D (Doubleday/Avon)
Singing Black (Reed Visuals)
Jim Flying High (Doubleday)
The Day They Made Biriyani (Third World)

THEATER

River of My Song
Boochie
Portrait of a Man

MARI EVANS, educator, writer, musician, activist, resides in Indianapolis. Formerly Distinguished Writer and Assistant Professor, Africana Studies and Research Center, Cornell University, she has taught at Indiana University, Purdue University, Northwestern University, Washington University in St. Louis, the State University of New York at Albany, the University of Miami at Coral Gables, and Spelman College in Atlanta. She is the author of *Where Is All the Music* (1968), *Nightstar* (1981), and *Black Women Writers (1950-1980): A Critical Evaluation,* among other books. She is the recipient of a National Endowment for the Arts Creative Writing Award, a John Hay Whitney Fellowship, and the Hazel Joan Bryant Award from the Midwest Afrikan American Theatre Alliance. Her highly acclaimed *I Am a Black Woman* (1970), long out of print, will be reissued by Harlem River Press this fall.

A DARK AND SPLENDID MASS

BY MARI EVANS

HARLEM RIVER PRESS
New York / London

WRITERS AND READERS PUBLISHING, INCORPORATED
P.O. Box 461, Village Station
New York, NY 10014

Cover design by Janice Walker

Copyright © 1992 Mari Evans.

ISBN: 0-86316-312-2

Library of Congress Cataloging-in-Publication Number: 92-073425

0 1 2 3 4 5 6 7 8 9 0

Manufactured in the United States of America.

BROTHER, COMRADE, CONFIDANT

(For Hoyt W. Fuller, Jr., 1923-1981)
I
May 1981

Brother, comrade, confidant
the fabric of our lives is rent
How do we keep on keeping
without you our rugged rock
our cornerstone
How do we sing the song
with your indomitable voice
no longer lordly, no
longer loudly raised
How do we wage the wars
Where will we find the strength
in the absence of your sure concern

If you had known the measure
of our unrestricted grief
The bottomlessness your going left
That time could never heal our
anguish at your passing
Being you, you would have
put the day on hold and labored for
another lifetime yes to shield
all those who keen and mourn you
from this lacerating pain

Brother, confidant, and friend
the fabric of our lives is rent
We say your legend, even now
there is a rainbow of our tears
in full pursuit

II
August 1982

And now
this sudden quiet
your name whispered
it is not as though we loved you
not enough, but rather that our pain
is more than sanity
can bear do not believe
the myth that Time will heal
Time moves us on but
    single file
irrevocably
Alone

III
May 1985

Past colloquium and celebration
past academe and argument
and you, yet unavenged
There is this chill crevasse
    this still abyss
down which our love stands looking

Brother, comrade, confidant
the fabric of our lives is rent
And in the absence of your sure concern
who has the strength and
which of us will say
"This, is the fine
direction"?

Contents

Search

Fog-blind
pain-directed
  nerve ends raw and
  contact bruised
    One
wanders
through the Life-mist
    hands outstretched

Modern American Suite in Four Movements

I New York City

The diamond lights, the glitter, all the jazz
    the Symphony
  the midnight blue and amber stages
  pristine ballet boys and girls
   the fashionwise professionals
  garment racks in noontime flight
   All these are but periphery

The Truth, the crux, remains
the restless non-essentials
  insistent
  ambulatory
Prowling crowded corridors
Crusted ankles scabbed and sore
Seekers after sustenance
Headfirst in wells of wanton waste
Connoisseurs of gourmet garbage
Gluttons seldom filled and never
satisfied   decay and rot a sauce
for hardy souls who wage with death
a never-ending war   This
is America
     to me

And still the spirit lives
A thousand tongues however torn
sing wild insouciant refrains
Cacophony of doggedness, of dried
            of withered dreams
Locked in desperate struggle these
            the Giftless
      still possess the power
        to Give:
For they defy all logic save
the Will-to-Be, the Will-to-Live and
      counter to all circumstance
      resist with tensil obstinance
that most seductive intermittent urge
        to yield and die

      And ultimately triumph!
      Only they and God know why

II Bag Ladies Sleeping

Their femalebodies hug the floor
Their many-layered legs are greyed and
greasy
    poulticed
Their bruised and battered shanks lie
    marrowcold and still seeking
      succor from the night
        they come
for death in many guises owns the streets
They gather here, crème de la crème
The fortunate   first-in-place
at public shrines to defecation
compelled by one deep need: To disappear
into some private place where one's own space
though commandeered is owned
However soiled and spotted even stench
is better than the night's
sadistic fingers

      Their femalebodies hug the floor
compelled by some imperative
  to disappear, all memory refused
      into some private place

Then from the chalice of their common need
eyes closed, each cloistered in her own
      cold isolation
See them say the white tiled beads
      Watch
            while they commune

4

III As the Dusk Begins Its Stalking

The camelcolored coat and widelegged slacks
generic middleclass, an aging decade's fashion
Lady of the evening rush, defying memory
The light is red and with thee
A mindless faith will shield you from
   the rush, the green released
               the roar

She challenges the headlights, a battery aligned
Daring chaos, din, congestion
See! Her desperation stills the clamor, stuns.

Traffic held at bay and she
   the centering
Middleaged, from some suburban Neverland
Fear in every crease and furrow
Making homelessness an issue;
Homelessness, once distant horror
      now a grotesque
   walking through the world

Watching Past confront the Present
puts tomorrow's pledge and promise
in more imminent perspective

Once proud lady of the suburbs
Daring dusk and evening traffic
Primed by fear and desperation
and with very little forethought

5

Vestiges of yesterday's gentility
untarnished   Walks
   directly into headlights
Walks directly to the windows
Whispers an apologetic   Please

Would you good people be so kind
I have no place to
                sleep tonight
And I seem somehow to panic as
the dusk begins
       its stalking

See her Sign the Cross and bless each car
      And place her gift
        a kiss
   Two grateful fingers on the back of
      every donor's hand: A
       fair exchange

Then she in camelcolored coat
a fading decade's widelegged slacks
moves on thru din and asphalt dust
toward other lights and other doors
Each step a   non-decision
   As the dusk begins its stalking
   And as she awaits

          the night

III Entitlement

them muthuhfuhyuhs think they baddd
Ah'm bout as badd as them . . . say
"GET up off th' floor
can't even find a place t'piss.
Don' wont t'move?
I say awright jes lay there.

  Whoooooooosh!"

A Lace of Perforations

There comes with ultimate despair a time
of thin decision, empty options: I can
break out
blast the damned thing in or
separate the gauze and guff of Life
the gall, the bitter stuff of Life
the tears, I've had enough of Life
and slip serenely through
But anguish intervenes and
there are things to feel

We desperately
want to stay but O the bones we loved
transiting plane have left
a lace of perforations
How they wait, a splendid company
but incomplete

We feel the way
blindfolded,
hands outstretched
ambivalent
Touched with fine reluctance
Afflicted by some stubborn heart that
hums of sunlight after struggle

Denies death its frayed solutions sways
to ancient obeah rhythms still
    residual
        unsuppressed
    penultimate survival songs

Despite trauma, despite discord
despite any torn confusion
  wells again the need transcendent
  claim the Right-to-Live
  claim fiercely
     and stay

    To Sing
    sing, strong!

1 Have Not Ceased To Love You

I have not ceased to
love you nor to
care but
I have found a flame
elsewhere
and seem compelled
seem overwhelmed in fact
with laughter, witty repartee
and wine

So let me dance
until my wings are singed
(it takes no time)
Be patient with me love
do not despair

I have not ceased to love you
Nor have I ceased
to care

Lee Morgan

His blue yearnings   his
hoarse staccato screams a
stratospheric reaching
    pristine flight,
     A personal anguish, naked
     and intense
        Her single shot
antiphonous
          His love
blasted into some abyss
Elusive as any grace note he
could not be possessed
His last round breathing
poignantly on key
reverberating into infinity
the disbelief the silence
The held note's echo gone
The wooden platform's dust
       a gentle settling
     A reluctant tag

   discordant
    final

Music as Heartbeat and Blood

There have been men
intimate with arpeggio
with the citrus sting of cymbal
with the whirr and wisk of brush
who were themselves soft sensuous nightsongs
haunting and haunted
                formidable
the pulse intense and complex
daysongs reworked
            hour on disciplined hour
Men whose eyes were early evening fires
   dangerously banked
               lashed with longing
Men who sang persuasive lovesongs soft on
alto saxophone on flute and Fender
fingers copper, lean, coercive

      Men whose other instruments were those
  of tenderness of feathered touch
          natural phrasing
etudes throbbing through quiescent
sunlit afternoons   pregnant classics
          creative voicing, pristine
            bass overripe throated
The stroll arrogant and dominant

thirty two measures then one note
extended breathing
                    circular
                              a linear bursting
         A virtuoso performance

Lemon-Honey Man

Sometimes the mind requires and
love lets go but O
your lips I will remember
lemon-honey man

And to be pinioned by,
to be enclosed and gentled by
your lyrical steel thighs is
ancient ritual performed, is
fragrances released, the holy
tendersweet exchange
To say each others' language
is a Celebration.

It is far too much
to walk away

Sometimes the mind requires and
love lets go
But for this time, for now
it is the whisper of your lips
I will remember
lemon-honey man

The Catalyst

You smiled
and I dropped everything
to follow
But even as we walked you
smiled
at yet another
And there I was
bereft of all I'd owned
before you smiled at me
and led me on
Now how can I go back
and be content
With the nothing
that I had
before I went

Amtrak Suite 1

(A Dark and Splendid Mass)

Crevasse and mountainside a
dark and splendid mass, cloaked
    and threatening; a forest armed
      veterans at attention
dense, close ordered, impenetrable
The valley sister to the ravening gorge
a fading light, the lengthening shadows. There atop
the distant rise a silvered saucer
imaged in the eyes of does
           Albino does
  a motion in the mind
The dusk drifts down
    The evening news, silt
whispered in cadence
    from another planet

Amtrak Suite II

(Passing a Penitentiary, in Full Flight)

The train in flying gear rocks past a flat red prison complex
Urged beyond its passions, its performances, to flee
the elongated fingers straining at escaping windows

Forced to race in futile contest it will neither place nor win; with
stark and fleshless dreams in swift and shifting pursuit; with
chill imaginings and opaque eyeballs prying through the clouded
thermal panes—See the train in flight, it speeds the bedrock
past untidy undergrowth and past the ragged stands of pine

Red brick walls cannot contain the narrow, barren lives, they
have no baggage and are faster than the whine of
late November wind. They lie in wait within the cages
nails unsheathed and hunger honed; a mass
undisciplined and eager, passage subsidized, their
destination of no real import for 'there' is anywhere but here
The instinct, the insatiate goal, the pure intent:
To ride-a that train each time
each time   each time   each time
      each   time

Amtrak Suite III

(Fading Orange Sunlight on Deserted Ruins)

It speeds her on to where no one is waiting
Where no hand will sweep the curtain to one side nor
lift the shade a bit to peer beneath nor
crack the door to tilt the head out and inquire
of the street. The train is in control
     of Time and Situation
She is scrunched, an emptiness, a
Woman in a corner watching trees rush backwards
Caught in some relentless forward movement
Her reluctance no concern at all

It speeds her on, this train
that gives so little and imposes much
     It speeds her on
   to where no hand will sweep the curtain
   to one side nor
   lift the shade
   nor tilt the head out to
   inquire
   of the street if

   she is near
   or
     anywhere

The Heart as Canvas

See the heart as canvas, touched
with brush inscribed with pen
The heart as marble slab
assailed
the chisel unrelenting
See the heart as pulse
as bloodstream
bruised and panting
Mean to live
     Resolute
    Undaunted
      Steeled
        In spite of
         Yes.

       To live!

Celebration

I will bring you a whole person
and you will bring me a whole person
and we will have us twice as much
of love and everything

I be bringing a whole heart
and while it do have nicks and
dents and scars,
that only make me lay it down
more careful-like
An' you be bringing a whole heart
a little chipped and rusty an'
sometime skip a beat but
still an' all you bringing polish too
and look like you intend
to make it shine

And we be bringing, each of us
the music of our selves to wrap
the other in

       Forgiving clarities
    soft as a choir's last
     lingering note our
      personal blend

I will bring you someone whole
and you will bring me someone whole
            and we be twice as strong
                    and we be twice as sure
and we will have us twice as much
        of love
                and everything

Ode To My Sons

I am the vessel from whence you came
the lode filled with imaginings
aside from dreams my longing cannot
touch your reaching nor can I direct
your quest
      Your center is the earth the
cool continuum of mountain stream
the blasting winds
Nor can I follow there for I
am but bound flesh from whence you came
My private griefs are private griefs
and you will have your fill of such
I wish you joy and love and strength
a centering of mind and will
a homeward journey to your core
and when chaotic winds subside

    an overflow of peace
       a quiet soul

Eulogy for a Child Whose Parents Prate of Love

Listen to his song
This child
This singer without voice
This solitary figure
on the barren plain of life
A dislocation
Rife with chlorophyll for
One last melancholy spring
Listen to his voice
This singer without tongue
Without significant thrust or timbre
Disconnected   he has met
The threshing winds
Unclothed, full-faced
With no sure understanding

If some protective sun could just
Embrace him

He would live

Who Is It Will Not Bend?

There is a law, but somehow it is always
    her word standing shamed
   against his sober protestations
    She an imprecise eleven
   dusty braids haphazard sprouts
   who knows her mother's head
    or could say why?
So much to do, so little time or need
   to intervene on her behalf
Our Corinne of the bony limbs
    the willful braids
    the yardwide smile
  the mote in Mr. Tony's eye and he
The guest who came one month for dinner
    Who forgot to leave
  Whose thoughtful eyes bought four
     young sisters
      See!
A portion of his Friday pay for rent
   with bags of food
   with Jim Beam for their mama

   And Willasteen
The best deal of her life to date
   a pleasured amber warmth
   the sure oblivion
    Drones one refrain:
But that was only play and only love and
only love and only play and did not hurt

he meant no harm
No go on back in there now leave me 'lone
Corinne

How classic this collusion: This
partnering of weakness with
the quiet steel of evil
We the co-conspirators
consenting by our silence
Refusing still to interrupt the chosen
rhythms of our lives
rhythms of our lives
Although we mourn her smile we do not need
to know her name
We do not choose to know her name
We do not want
to know

Who knows her mother's head?
Or ours?
And who will scream the words?
who will fight the fight?
who will guard the child?

Who is it will not bend?

How Sudden Dies the Blooming

(For Paula Cooper and all the other children on death row, cir. 1989)

How sudden dies the blooming
An instant's crass confusion
      An err of hand
   and heart and head
A bent decision then
          and now
one instant in the past as
   constant present
Rarely out of reach the act
Tethered to some unrelenting
         infinite recall
   Today's reality
in yesterday's precise and fine
          detail
One moment's cruel confusion
carved forever in the spirit's
    tender steel
How sudden dies the blooming
How withered lies the promise
   lies the reach
      the blind potential
  All that lingers in the breathing

is a warp of understanding
a fist of clear confusion
and a desperate
      a frightened
           need
    to live

Limited Aggression

O there are lands
    and in them
one-armed children watch
        horror-stilled
eyes lasered past any
acknowledgment
    motionless   they
are not moved by   wind
Wind seamed with death
caterwauling a wild anguish

Violated widows twist
soil ragged hems
their bony fingers
a forgetfulness

They will stare forever
down the dusty
       vacant
         road

Through a Glass

Blackbonneted the eager
Amish child
peered through glass
fingers seeking and cold
caressing and cold
eyes quick and curious
urged on by some surging will-to-be
peered through the plate glass door
and pushed and pushed
until defeated claimed the floor
face down and silent
arms extended
overcome with failure

A peel of garments
black and brown and navy
Hatted blackbrimmed eyes
a row inscrutable and tender
unyielding as the cold mosaic floor
a disciplined rebuke
bathed her in an ancient
understanding

Chastened birds
with broken wings
they too
once sought the wind

1 Am Cut Off from My Memory

I feel mute before your pictures I
can but reiterate my love
                    And weep

I did not know that I contained these tears
or that I needed this release
from stalwartness
I am mute before your pictures
cut off from my memory
My who I am goes back
to who I was at five
But then I skip some

And they have told me what they know
but they must skip some
For all they know is what they heard
and those were tales that had no end
and parts were told in passing
headed up or down the river on the way
to somewhere else
                    Some nowhere clothed
in terror
            Yes!   Some white and red hole
      ice and fire
far from those specific tears

and laughter never heard again except
on lonesome nights beneath some mournful
moon or in the reaches of a sometime
dream
      Or in the mind

O I am cut off from my memory

They say Odugon people all
got big behinds and I
must be Odugon
Say you look like a Fulani
      in the face
Or like Masai or from the East
Grand Amy be half Cherokee
      Remember that.
Or someone else half Iroquois and
Blackfoot on y'Daddy's side

An Uncle Morris? Spittin image of them
blueblack Mollyglascoes
Say Odugon people all got big behinds
They eye each other and they look at me.
My who I am goes back to who I was at five
and only some of who we were Before
And I have had to coax and rail, to
lie in wait my ears afire
for all the rest.   O

I feel cut off from my memory

They have told me what they know and
     what the heart allows them
         to recall
But always   they must skip some
    For part of what they know is
       what they heard
      Tales told in passing
headed up or down the river on the way
      to somewhere else

A Rock for Sheltering

Child
with guilty darting
eyes
find surcease
in
my love and know
no cause
for subterfuge
nor hide
your troubled face
                    for
        Here I stand:

A rock for sheltering—
        Child
    take my hand

Let Me Tell You How To Meet the Day

Life to be explored
Love, an ambiance
a climate
a Self to be identified
clarified
outlined, free form
so there is room to breathe
Ordered
so that the growth
is
Upward
That is how we stand before the sunrise
arms outstretched

The Nonagenarian

His hand itself the autumn
leaf and he in his November
dried and sucking from the sun
a chilly heat
              the whispery winds
blow quiet odors past his teeth
    A package
       used and battered
old and brown he makes his way
    about the town
      a superior compassion

Oral History: Found Poetry

"The Bishop was a good man," my
Father filled with memory would say
"When he walked down Savannah streets
                    the trees
    bowed down before him"   or
"an you ain had no peaches, girly
till you had a peach from Georgia!" Then
"We usta go out in the fields an thump
to find the swectes melons
bust em, eat the heart, and
                    thow the rest away
"An everywhere you look
everyplace you look was pine trees
                    an red clay

        "I nevah took no stuff
from off no peckerwood
neither did m'daddy
nor his daddy before him
        "Nevah fought their wars
nevah joined they army
neither me nor my daddy
nor hius daddy
nor his daddy before him
        Nosiree bob!"

"Sometimes we leave   Go up to Memphis
  Chattanoga, Knoxville, East St. Louis

"Sometimes we stay
  figurin out a way to fight'm back

"Y'great grandfather Reese was lynched
just outside Atlanta
N'they run y'uncle Morris outa Macon
Yet and still, we nevah took no stuff

"Neither me nor my daddy
nor his daddy before him

"They sorta knew how we was
    and most ingenerally held back
    Long as they could, that is.
    Or till they brought some in t'help 'em"

Man Came Knocking

Man came knocking
I said "Who?"
He said "Ingram"
"Ingram, who?"
"Robert Ingram"
Dont know you"
He said "I'm
    a minister."
I said "Lawd, today!
I'm busy."
So he went away.
I was by myself
Door locked.
    these men!
If he'd said he was the
laundry man

I woulda let him
in   Just dont
trust
no preachers

Liberation Blues

Woke up this morning, feeling sad and blue
I woke up worried, feeling sad and blue
Thinking 'bout my baby
And what he's put me through
Thinking how he done me
How he put me down last night
Thinking how he done me
He didn't do me right

Didn't fix no breakfast, had no appetite
Couldn't eat for thinking
How he hurt my heart last night
Thinking how he done me
He didn't do me right

I get up early in the mornin
Work hard each and every day
I bring home all my money
An yet he play
Ho ho pretty daddy, hurt my heart last night
Thinking how he done me
He didn't do me right

Reached for my work clothes, hangin on the rack
Then I decided I would put them muthus back

Thinking 'bout my baby
How he put me down last night
Thinking how he done me
He didn't do me right

Called and got a reservation
Kiss this house and him goodbye
Got me a reservation
Kiss this house and him goodbye
I don't have to stay and take it
I don't have to stay and cry

Never thought I'd leave him
Never believed the day would come
But this is not the first time
My baby's done the things he's done
Cryin shame the way he done me
All a y'all there last night
Saw the way he done me
He didn't do me right

I'm gone.

Ladies Waiting in the Mall

They refuse to know the name
these parchment ladies
no longer striding in some
social arrogance secure
in gown and guarded graciousness
     They refuse to know the name
     or recognize those faces
     once so grandly patronized
These powdered cafe au lait ladies
quiet now and shrinking
from the sear of public scrutiny
of Time revealed in pore and line and pouch
in the relentless obscene now
of thinning wave and nylon curl
     Preferring not to know a name
     these once tall ladies
     groomed and slightly fragrant
            slightly frayed
     wait in the glitz, the aimlessness
     of chic and failing shopping Malls
            for transport
Gone the grandeur once so carefully contrived

the firm if fragile flesh, the haughty stride
the unrelenting judgment, the clear demanding eyes
      All that remains
    a head averted slightly
    and a ragged clutch of pride

Rents Due Monday

The pervasive cold
    an icyfingered
                fire

Used to want a
    treehouse
             now
snowmist
invades my bed

Would heat th' kitchen
    with th' oven
        cept
    th' oven
    dont heat

Old mis pattons eyes
      blazed
between three sweaters
    two knit hats

Motionless
in the icy outer hall
        the junkie
            dreams
beneath the frostclouds
    of his breathing

The consuming cold
   searing
      pervasive
         possessive

the rents due Monday

The Elders

With their bad feet
and thcir gray hair
and Amazing Grace how sweet the sound
cardboard fans
with a colored family seasonal
gift from Baker's Funeral Home
stirring heat and hallelujahs
No hiding place down here, son
I asked Jesus to change your name, child
Help me Jesus
through one more day
And, yesma'am, I dont mind working late
again and nosir, I'm feeling fine
it be a long time before you need a
younger man t'work this job
And swing low sweet chariot Lawd
somewhere there's a crown f'me
Be our heritage
      our strength
The way they moved from can to can't
preparing the way
thowing down the road
Say want you to have more'n I had child
Say be more than I am, go
Go where there aint no limits
See you standing at the top a that mountain

46

lookin down

With their bad feet
and their gray hair
bony symbols of indomitable will
having triumphed over Goree
endured the Middle Passage
survived cotton and cane
branding iron and bull whip
crossed Deep River into Canaan
strode through dust bowl and depression
Smiled through smoking Watts and
Newark, smoldering Detroit and
locked old arms with young to sing
surely We Shall Overcome

And now
be saying Walk Together Children
we went through the undergrowth
with only cane knives and we
cut it down to size
Fight the fight, wage the wars
and win
It's in y'blood

With their bad feet
and their gray hair
they be our heritage
our strength

Torn tents pitched
at the foot of the mountain
having moved from can to can't
they be our national treasure
they be
      our priceless charge

Coda

How we go down the long path
      singly

mewling pain the shriveled
flesh the sharpened knee
to lonely chest

      How do you feel mama
      you're looking fine mama

We go

      You feel like singing mama

down the long path

   O I went to the rock
   to hide my face
   The rock cried out no
   hiding place

We go
   singly

The Time of Plague Is on Us

The time of plague
edges blurred beyond all
recognition
one body here
         and there
a stinking carcass left
from yesterday
Odor of the furnaces
  we will not need to know:
a clarifying climate

Death powdering the naked
nostril fire
careening through orifice and artery
Straining lovers who endure but
cannot reproduce themselves
Perverse and grotesque deaths conceived
in greening mansions born
in steel and granite cages as
removed as clouds from clod and foliage
The time of plague
is on us brethren
clearly must we see
the unconfuted foe and save
our internecine battles
for the Spring

The time of plague
is on us
     Let us rally
to the hue, that comely ebony
by which we are defined, lest
we betray a legacy of steel and wisdom.
Know this truth:The atavistic whitewinds
      sweep our shores
And O   The time of plague
is heavily upon us

A Man without Food

Resolute
icon of the revolution
the leader of the people
stubborn and stony
faced the cameras

He had swallowed his spittle
and could not wet his lips
"A man without food" he said
his lips parched and cracked
"is an animal"

"A man without food is an animal"
he said, confronting the cameras
his lips dry against his teeth

Touch Your Finger to the Wind

Kinsmen
peel the opaque from your eyes
denounce the scented blossoms what
bouquet more delicate and deadly
Ours to be plucked and savored, what
delusive dreams
            A green oasis
quiescent in tumultuous sands
misty respite from the raging
      from the night
chill Black reality and we
the once essential non-essentials
now the mindless dispossessed:

We do not own ourselves!
        We do not claim
              ourselves

The white day curdles
sirens whine through whirling suns
See! Steel pomegrantes dropping at your feet
burst their purple gore it
is not tomorrow
This day and you
flailing arms and legs

captured in the fluid of your mind
slowed to a perfected motion
Touch your finger to your tongue
and test the wind your head
against the earth's pulse
Hear the thunder?

Inform and form yourselves
　　offensively
　　　　　　against the foe
　　There is still time

On Winning the Gold

**(Tribute to a Champion:
Mark Breland, c. 1984)**

Iron and steel
forged in ghetto furnaces
in cold chaotic streetscenes
Smiling a tight line
His mother's image locked
behind the clearview in his eyes

Star Spangled Banner furl!
O alien familiar refrain
Tryin t'change his mind
poignant notes crowding his air
slashing his heart till the blood run
Deceptive, abrasive, entrenched
against the somber Truth
of his raw life

He be his own man
doing it his own way come
hell or high water
Gold medal bright on wet
mahogany   neither he
                  nor his mama
showed teeth

Mass Burial

His left arm recalcitrant
eluding the gluttonous bulldozer
see it lazily aloft
in the noon's heat

He was always
    set in his ways

Found Poetry

(Winnie Mandela: Television Interview, 1988)

When I was in solitary confinement
  for seventeen months

(it is hardly anything to talk about)
People have lost their lives
in solitary confinement

Alabama Landscape

(In Memoriam) *

I

See the ancient underbrush
the disciplined entanglement
wild welt of trees and gullies
traps of mud and broken branch
the hairline brook, the secret water
see the stirring, see him coming
modulating thru the silence
leaping sinkholes, torn confusion
buckling knees then grace regained
he ducks and dodges
                    Black man running
    claiming Freedom
thru the ageless sun and shadow
vanishes from sight he is at once both
Past and Present, history repeated
        history relearned

II

History relived

* For all the Black victims of "police action" lynchings throughout the United States, and especially for Michael Taylor, aged 17, who "committed suicide" by shooting himself in the temple while sitting in the back seat of an Indianapolis police car with his hands steel-cuffed behind him.

the Present savagely contrived, the
Past still swollen, still unhealed and
    All transition merely language.
What was tar, and rope, and flame, was
      rape and scourge
        is magnum now,
   is unrelenting chokehole

     Sanctioned lynchings
       Still orgasmic

III

The time is surely near
when we reluctantly have learned
what lessons time intends to teach
And such intransigence as now
is veiled and hid we will release
When "for their thousand blows" return
      a thousand ten
However unannounced, the Truth is clear:
Until we stand, until we act
the murders, the oppression still
     the unabated war
    we seem unable to define
      goes on

Black man running
thru the ageless sun and shadow
   Vulnerable
      still unavenged

History repeated past all logic
Who is it bides the time and why?
    And for how long?
There will be no one left, for ovens

There Will a Time of Rising

though huge winds
    try the grass
and though each
               blade
lie flat
     there will a time
of rising
       come
when each
          slim green and tender
shaft
    shall stand resilient
          strength
fulfilled
  it upward thrust
  a tribute
to indomitable
will

Save One Bright Jonquil

The dank air
reeked of decay
of rotted wood
and dreams that never
dared   there
was no beauty to the place
save one bright
jonquil
     Determindly
alive   and smelling
outrageously
of
Hope